Greetings Fellow Art Enthusiast and Mythological Connoisseur,

Thank you for your purchase of my first coloring book. Your patronage helps me to continue to create.

Welcome to Ancient Greece, where the gods, heroes and creatures of myth are real and centaurs run wild. This volume contains the concept art for my series, *Sons of Apollo*, which is based on the combination of several stories involving centaurs from Greek mythology. For more information about the characters in this book, as well as their stories, please visit my website at: www.normasueoneil.com

Welcome to the herd!

Sincerely,

Norma Sue

Table of Contents:

1. The Alpha
2. Right On Target
3. Winning The Race
4. Hold On Tight
5. Mate For A Centaur
6. Flowers For Mother
7. A Stroll Through The Woods
8. Centaur's Daughter
9. The Ferryman
10. Playing Tag
11. Kentauris
12. Javelin thrower
13. The Picnic
14. The Last Apple
15. Centaur Family

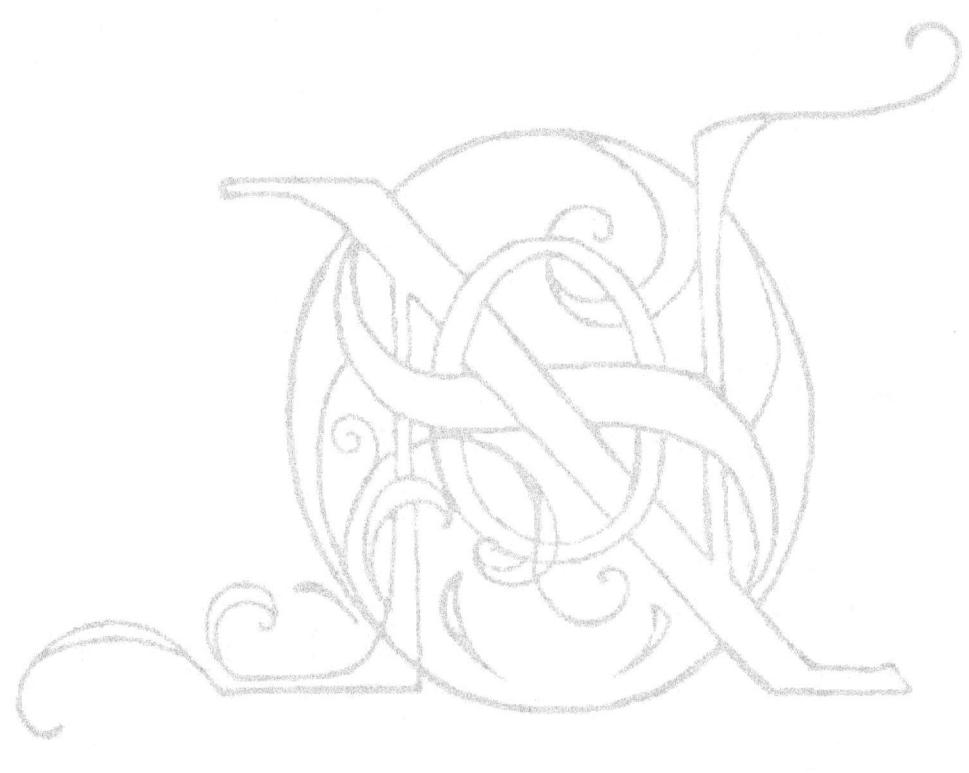

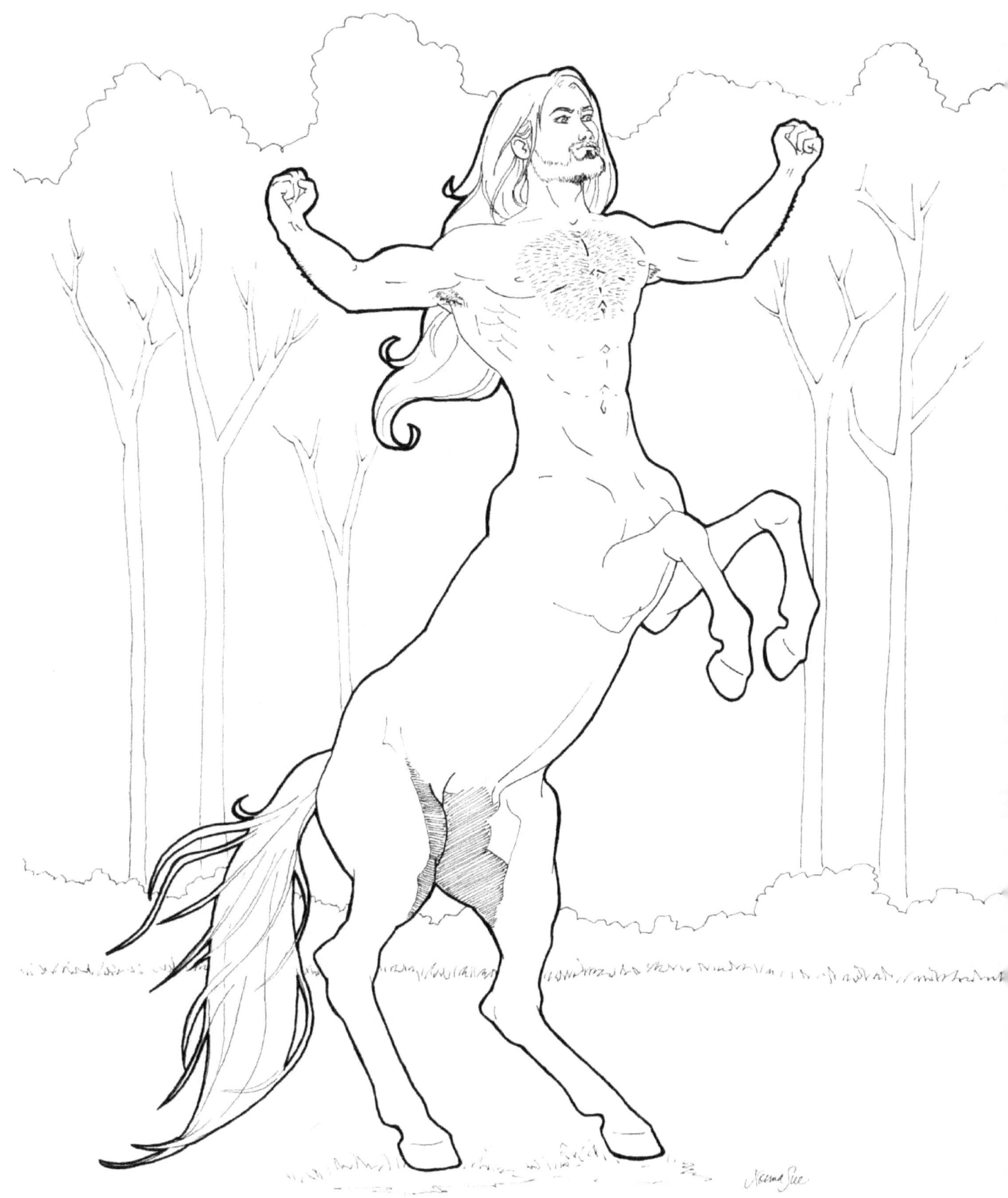

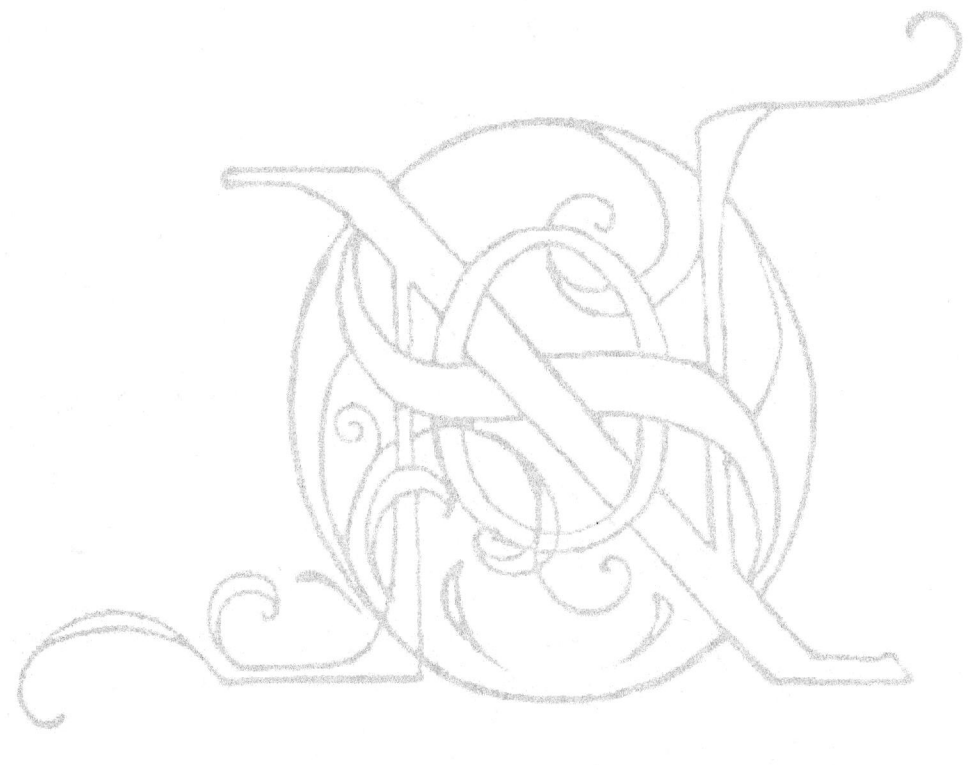

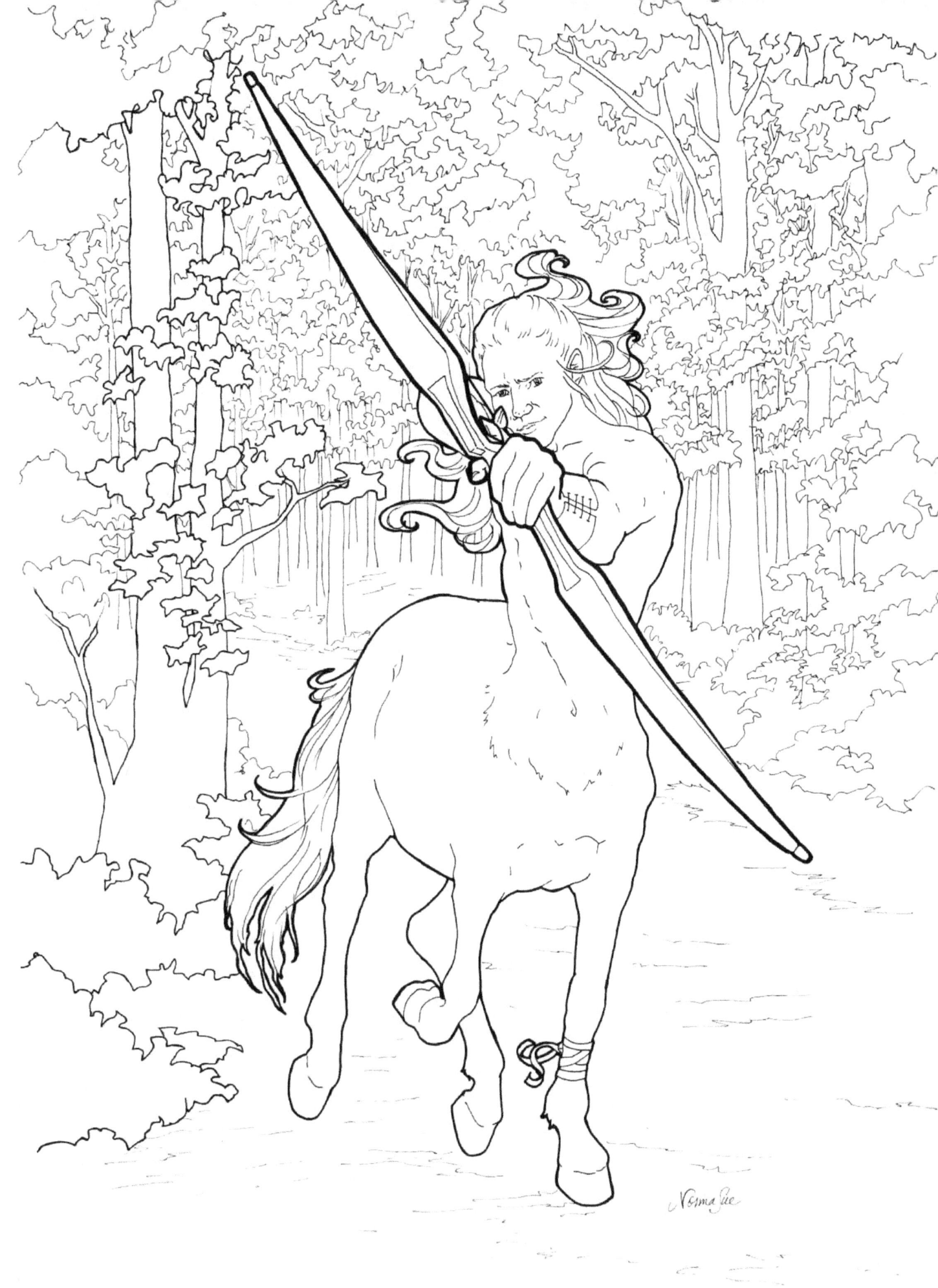

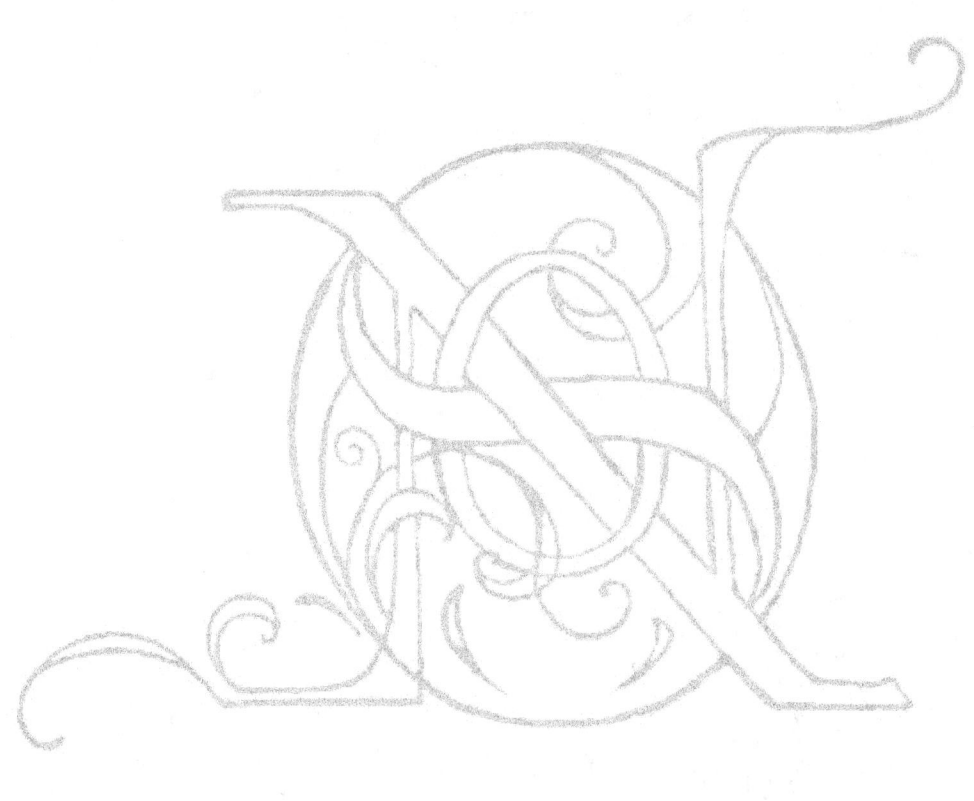

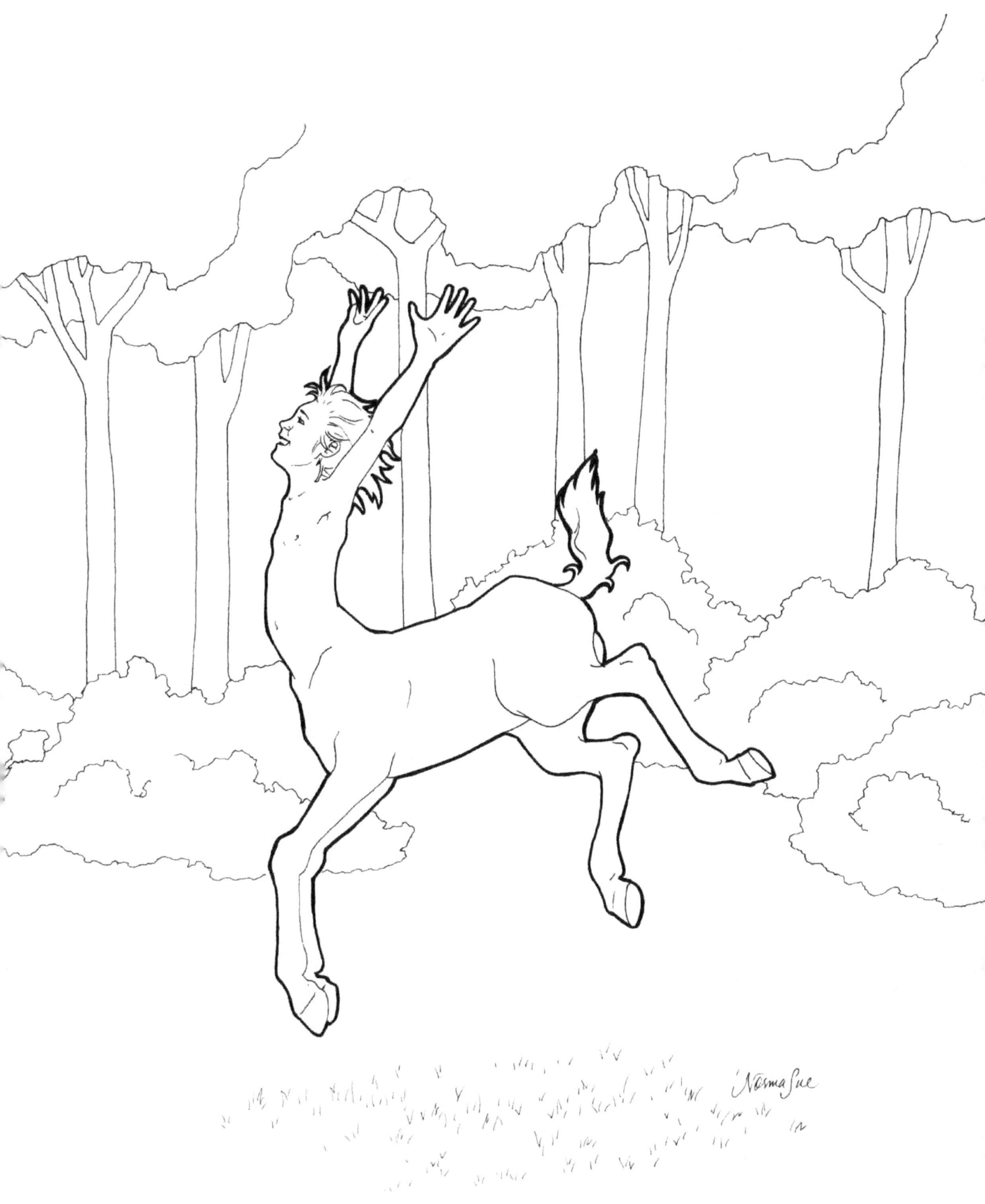

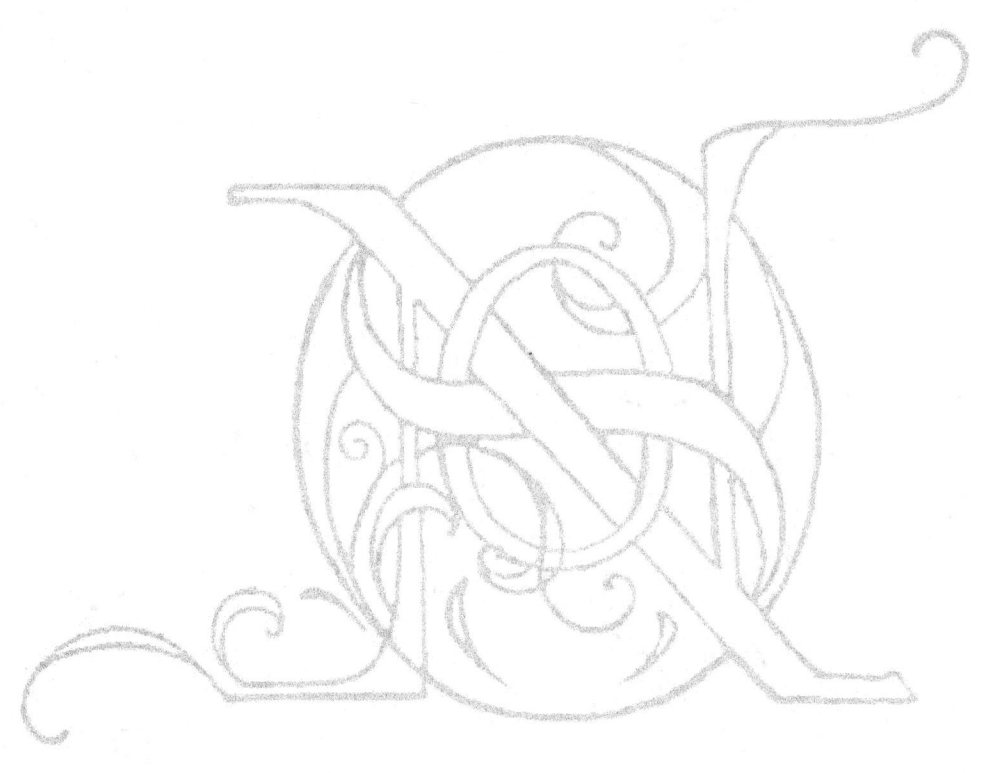

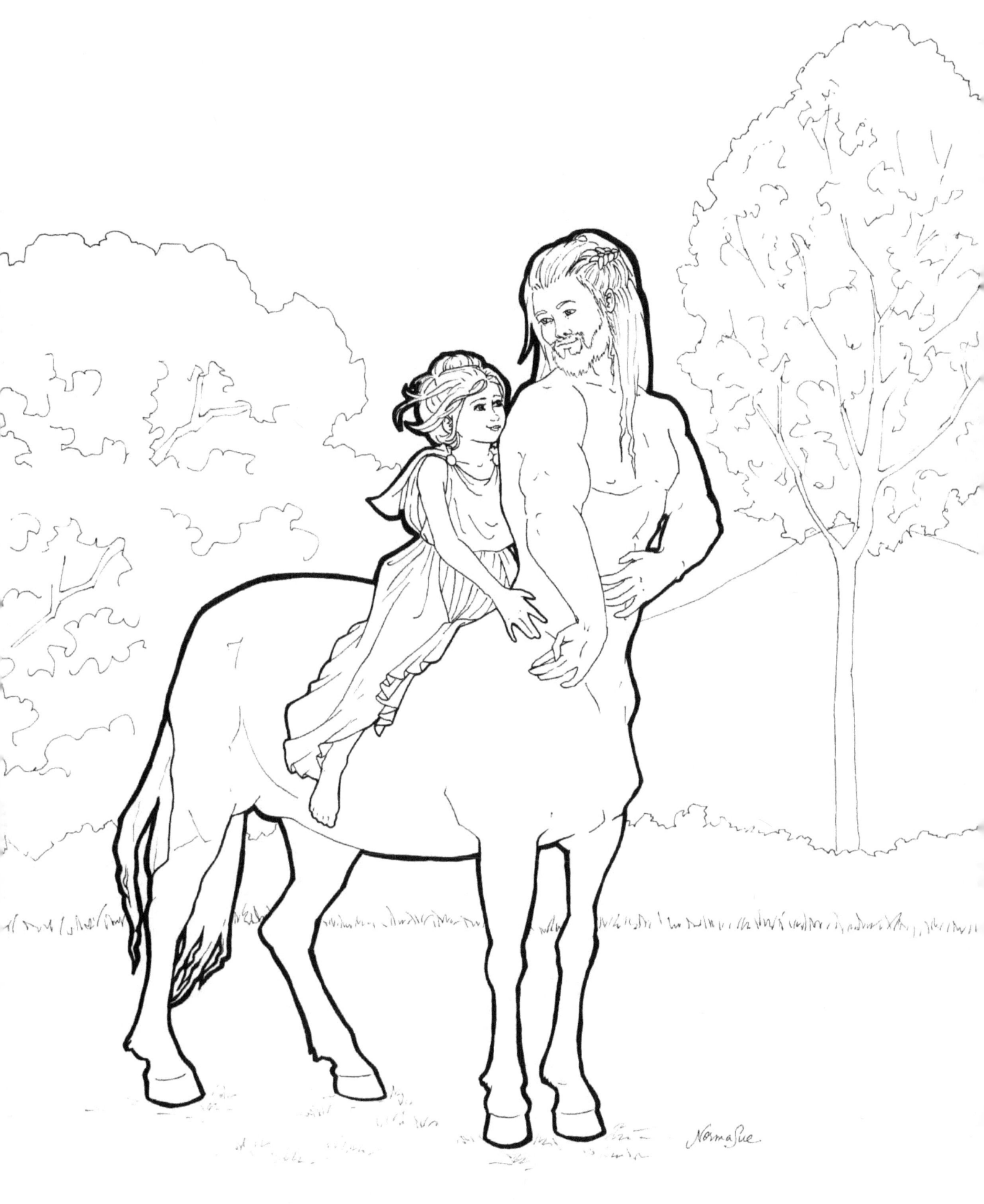

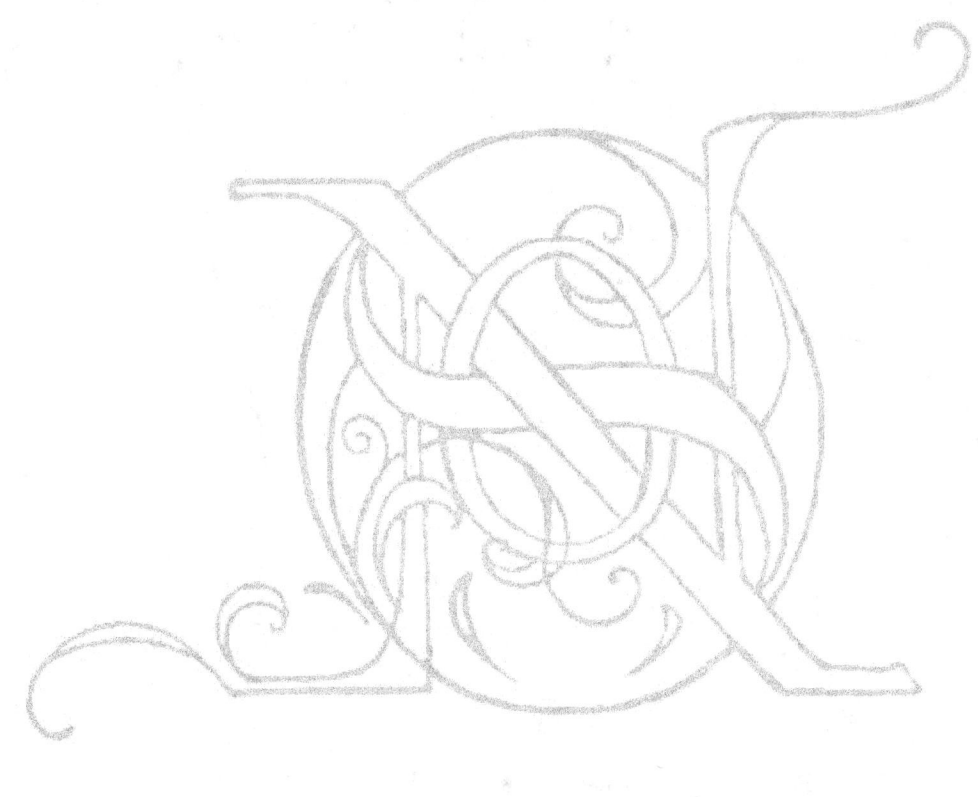

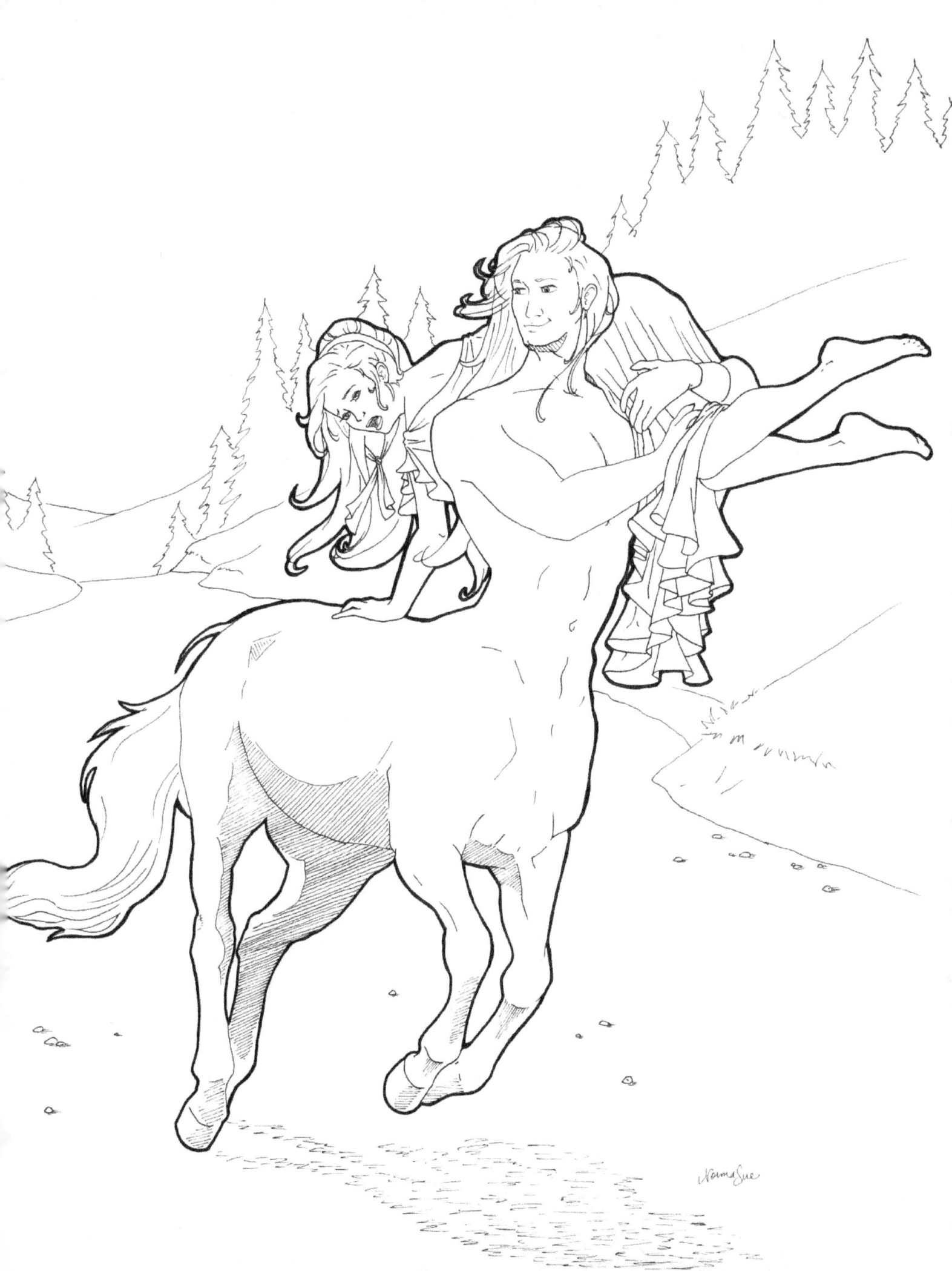

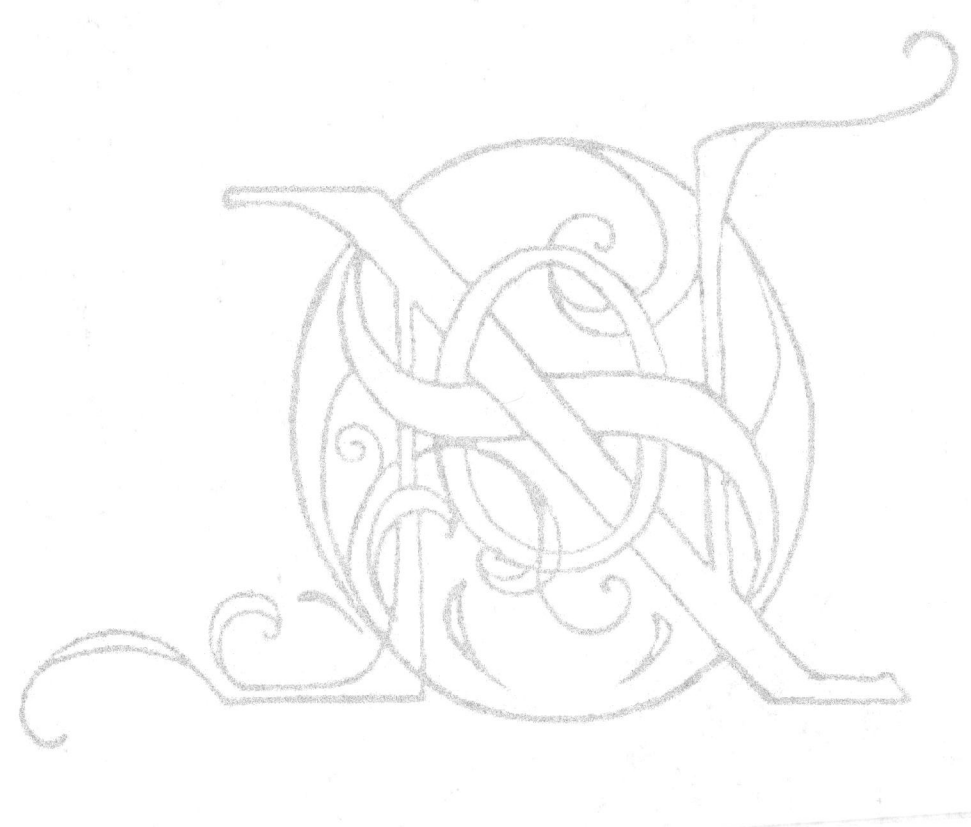

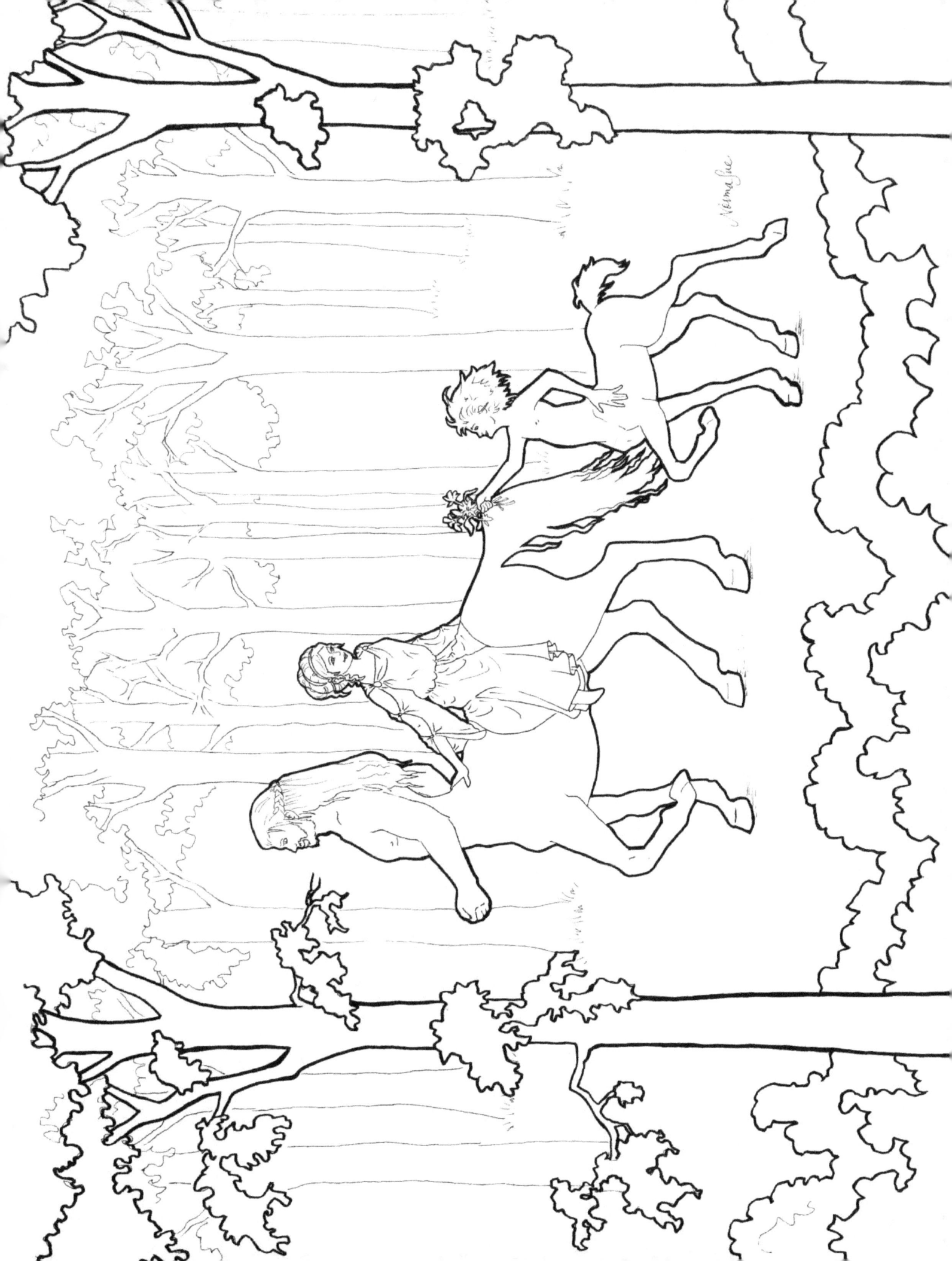

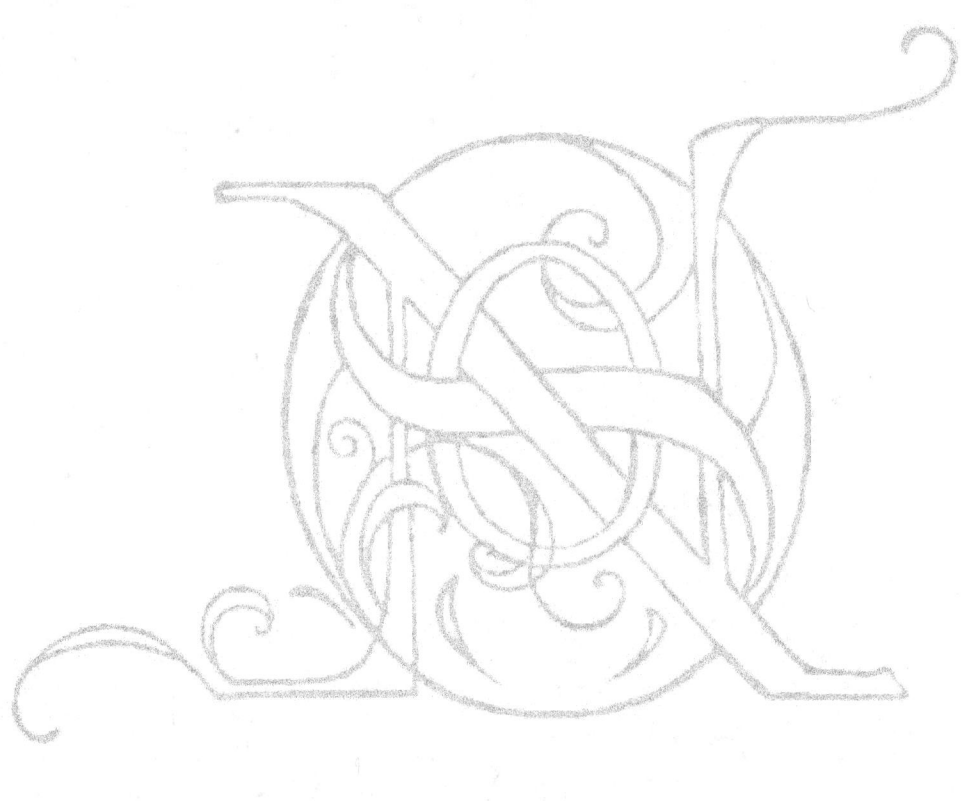

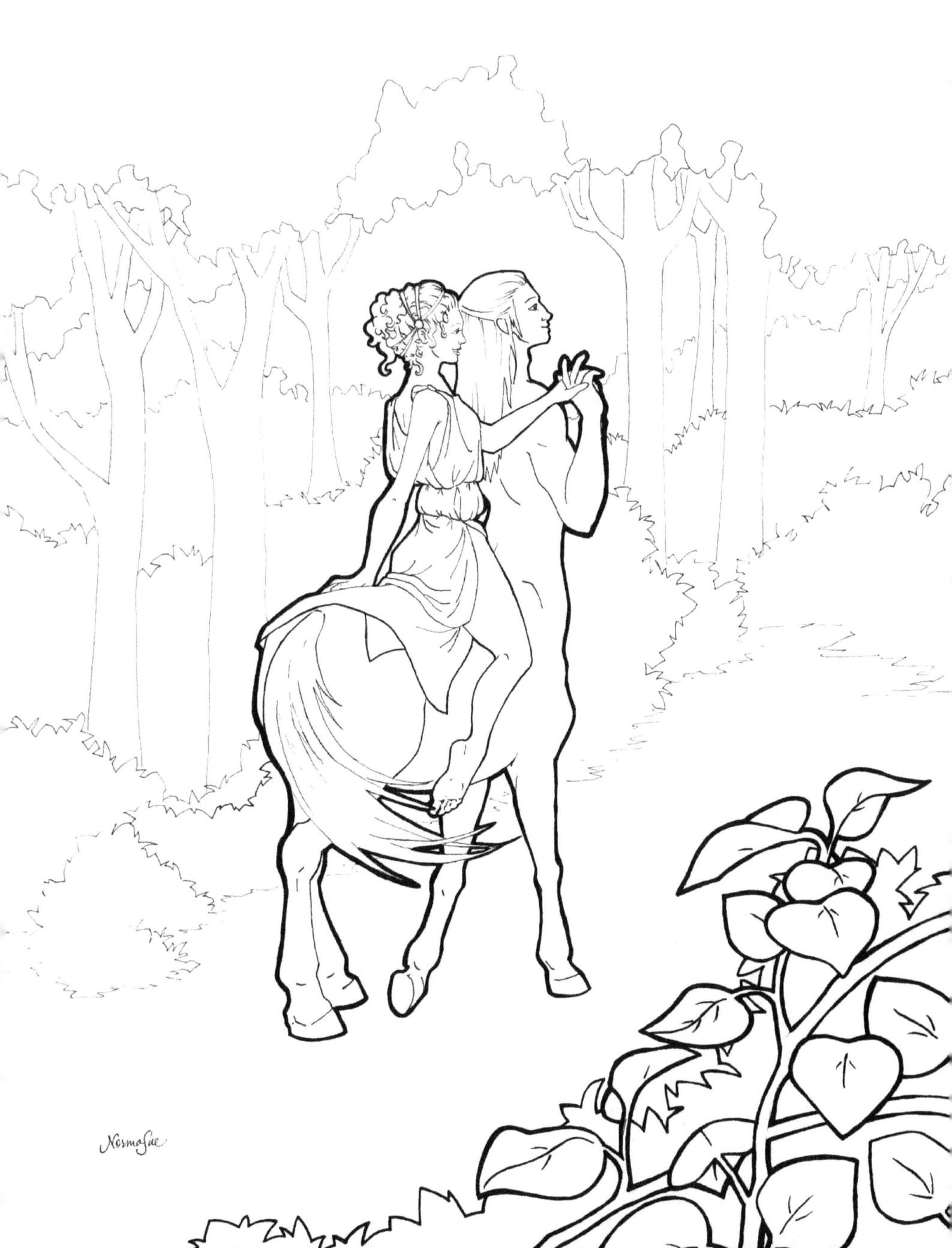

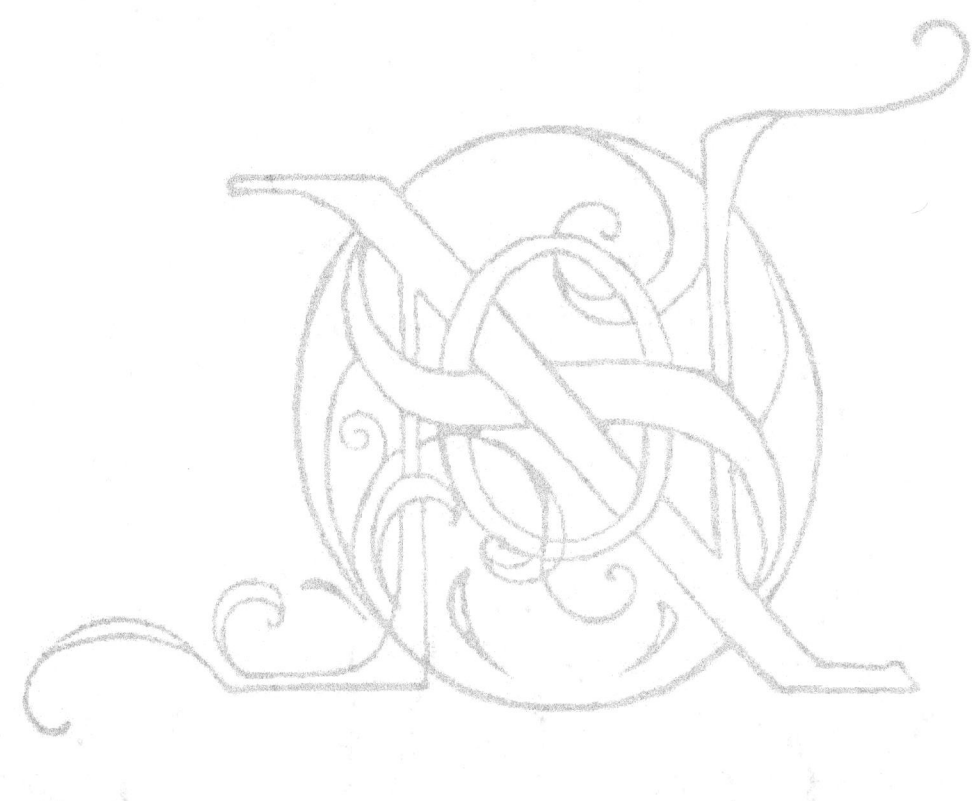

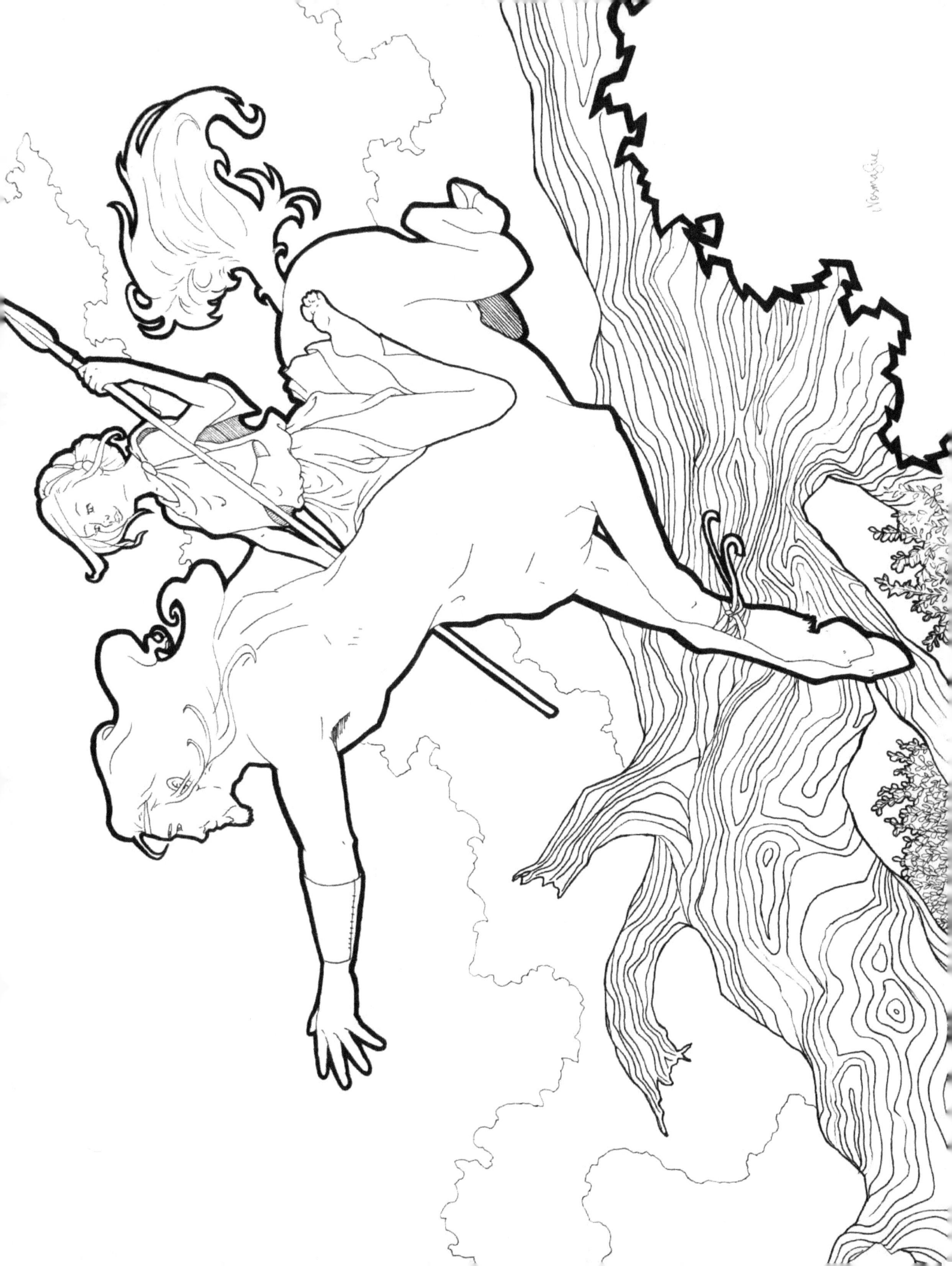

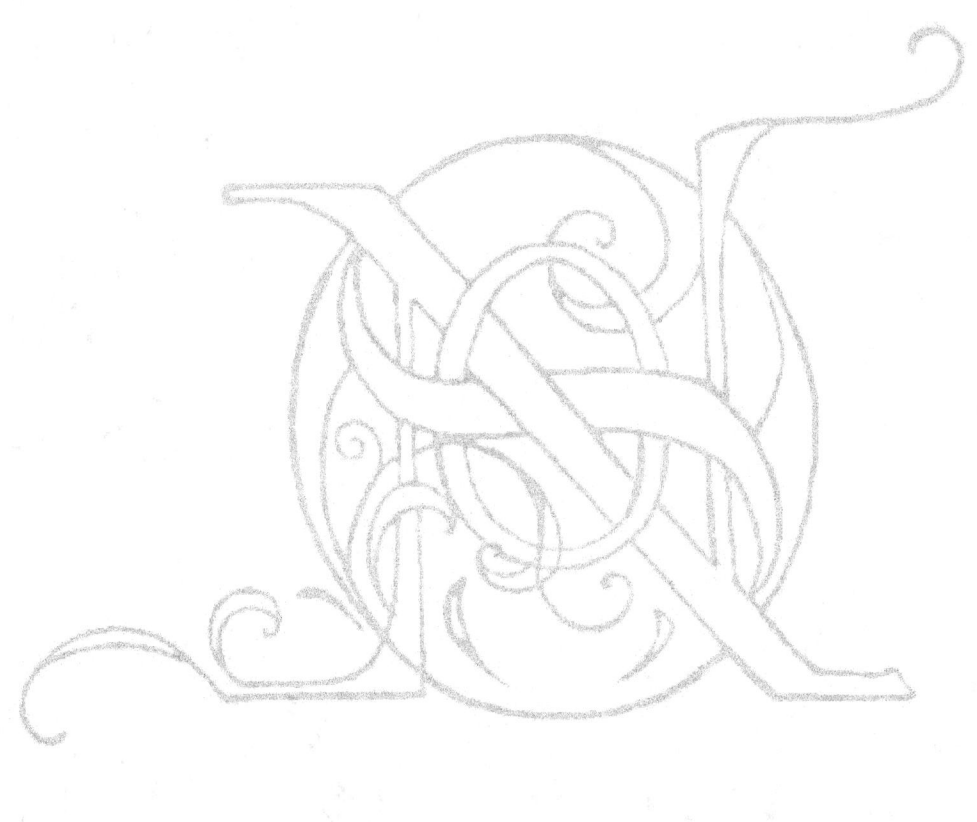

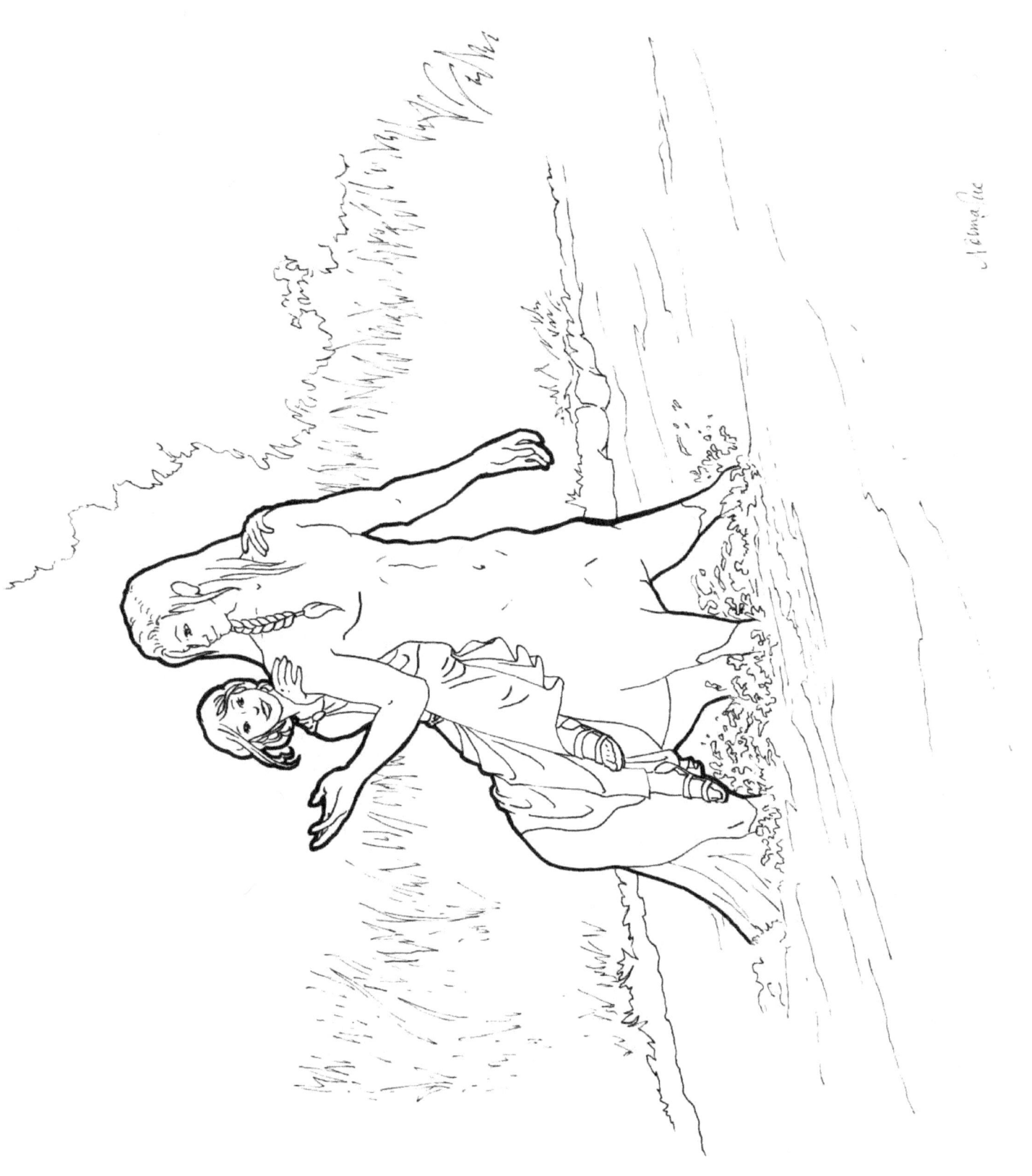

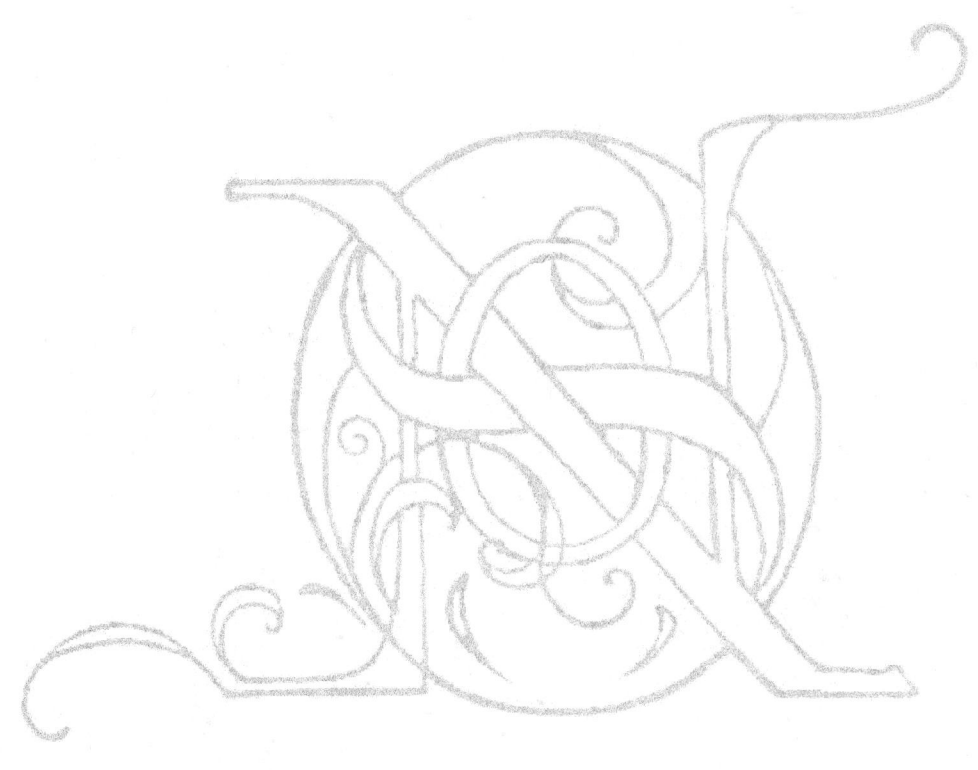

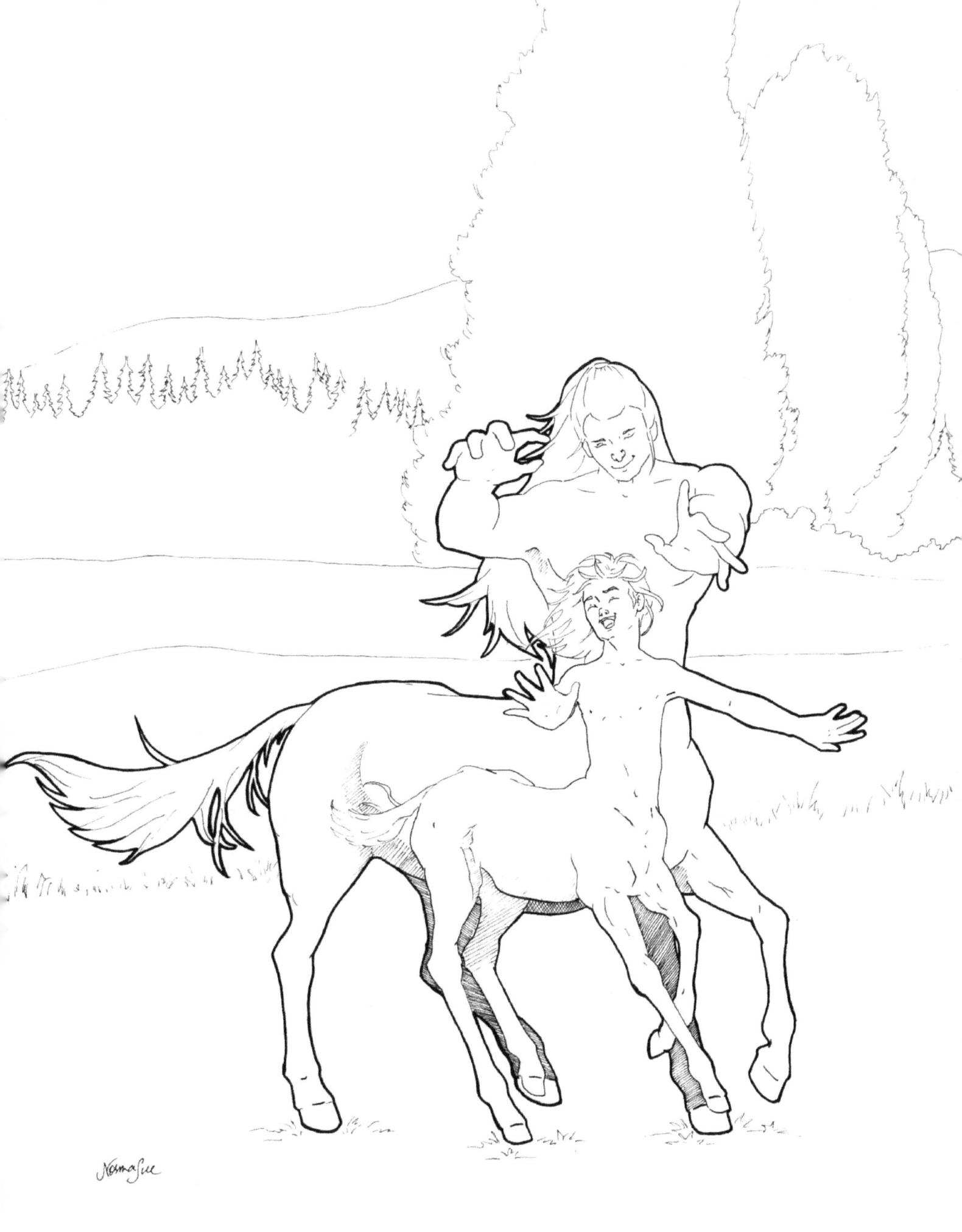

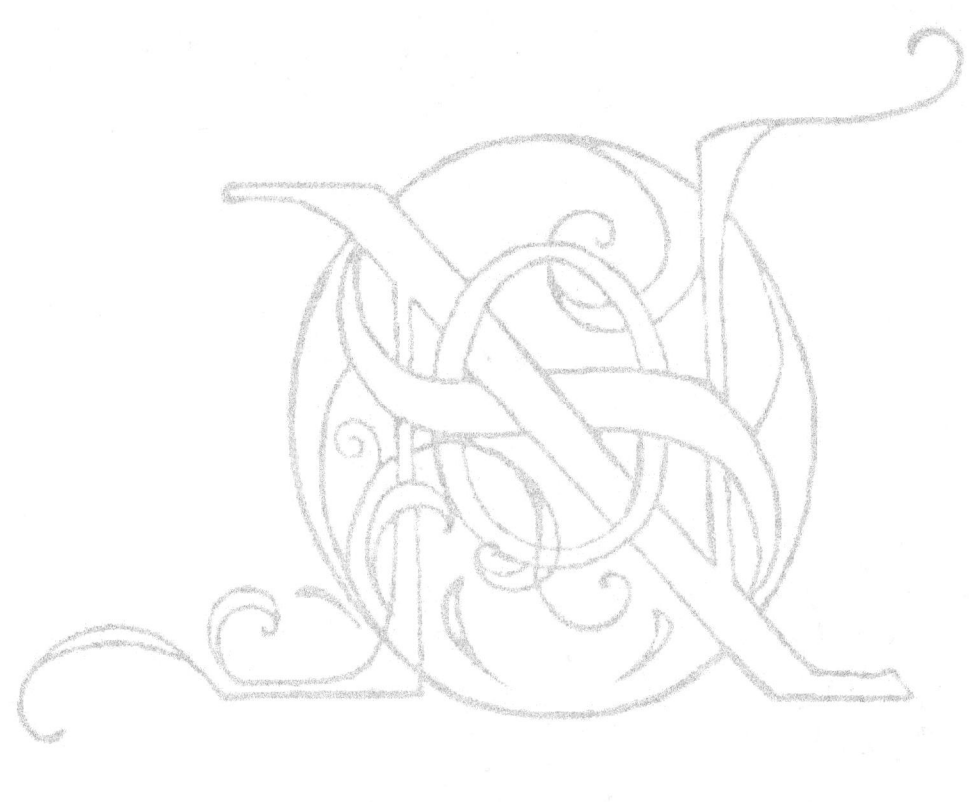

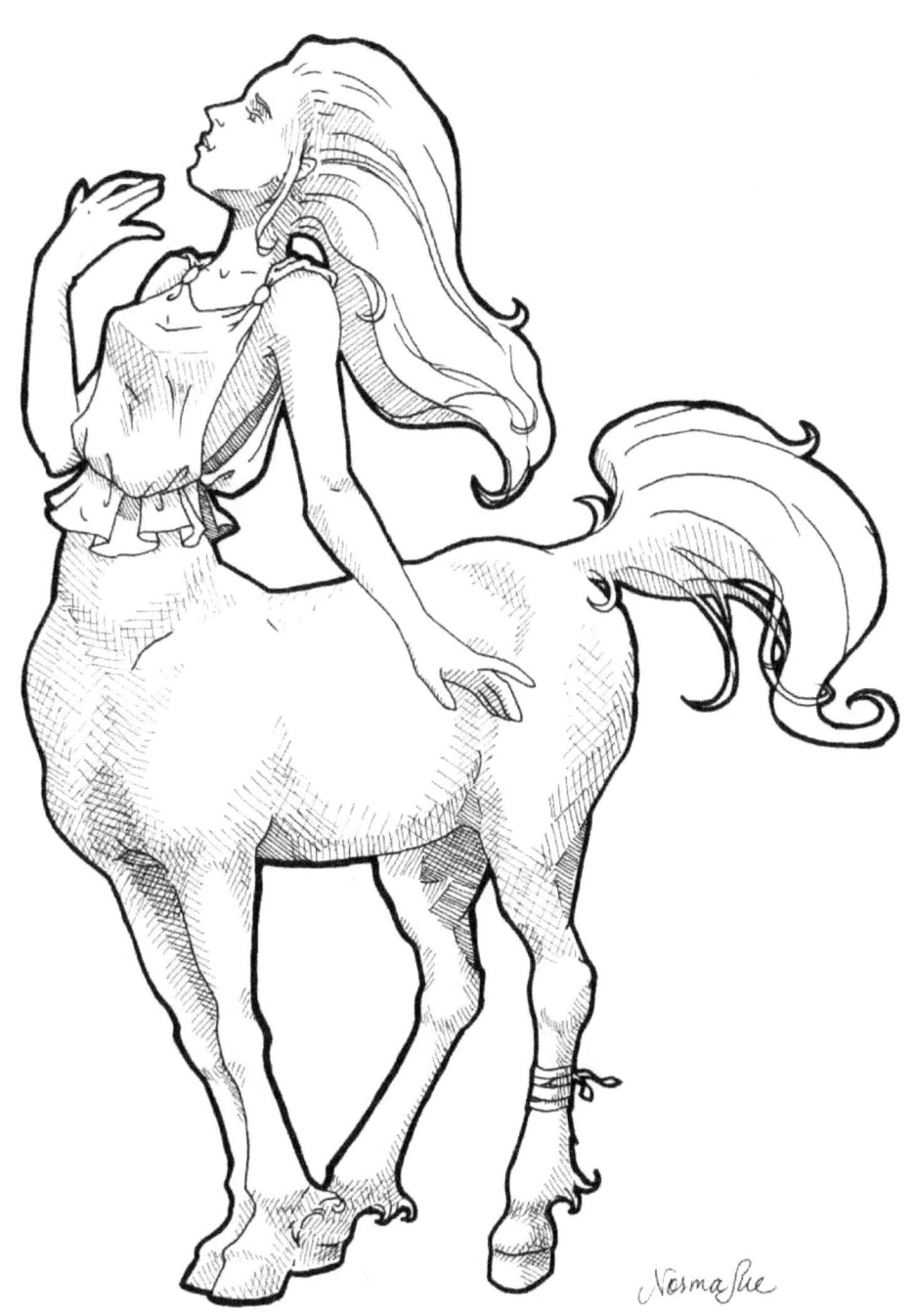

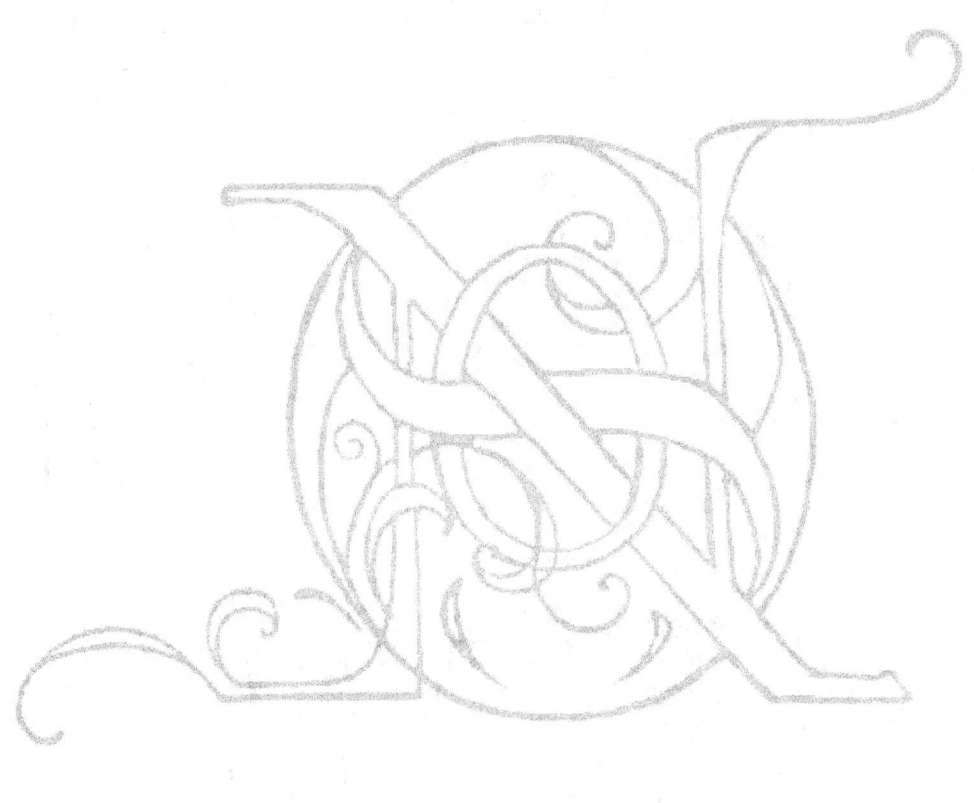

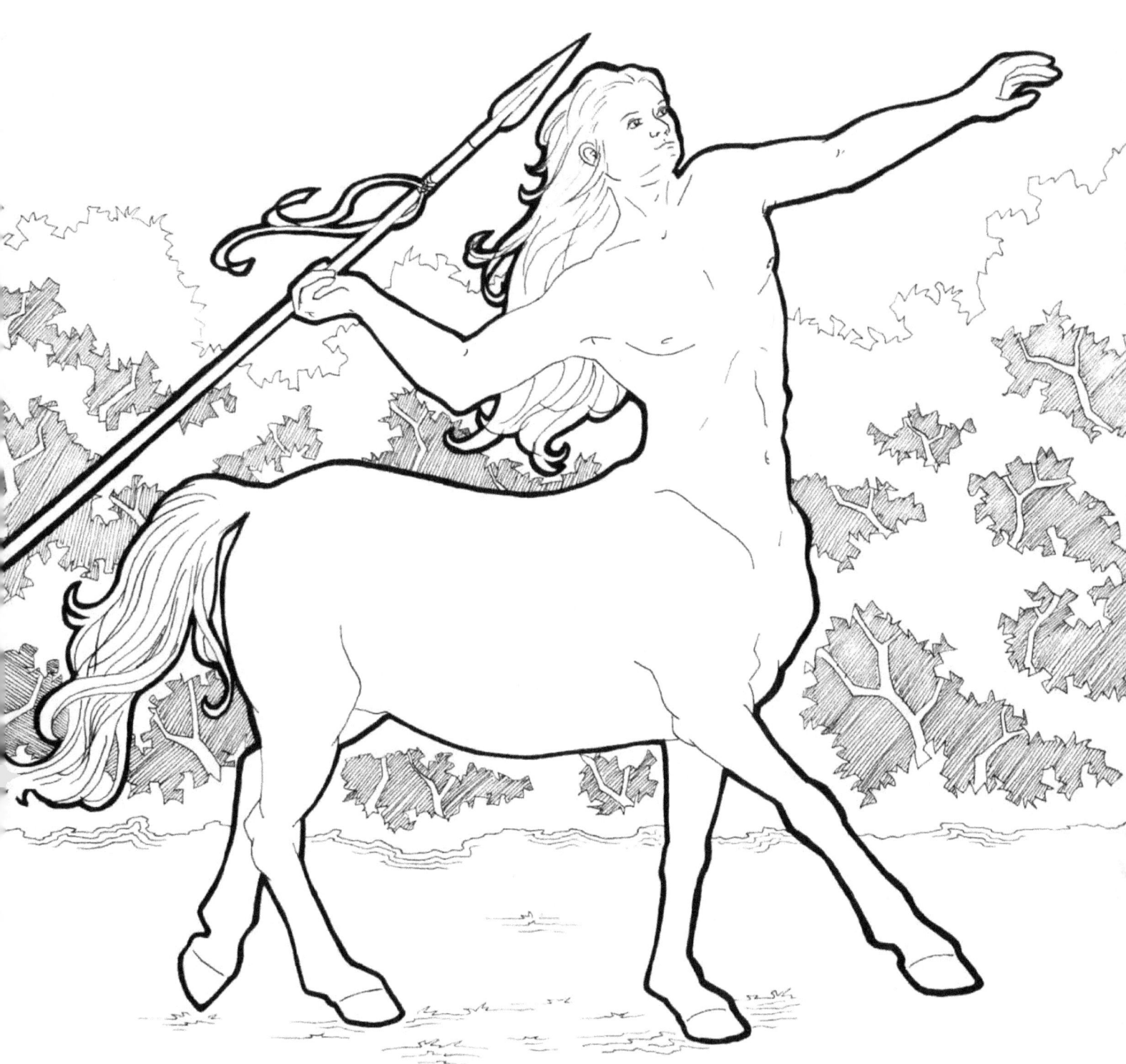

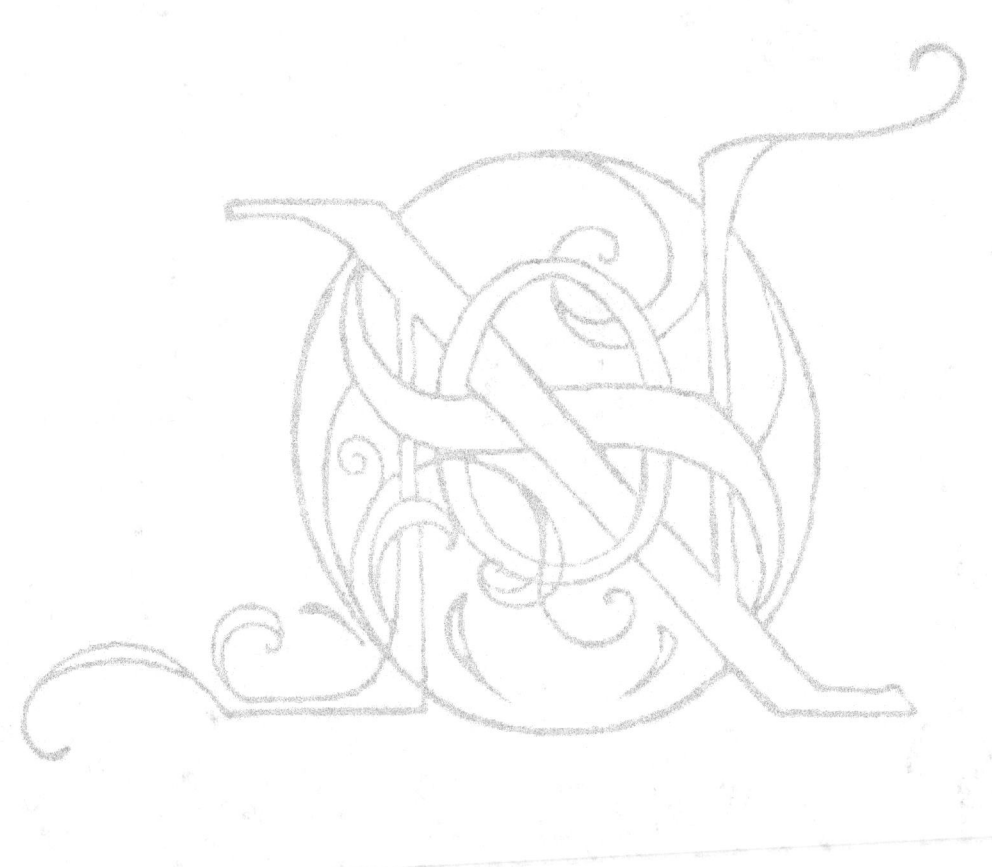

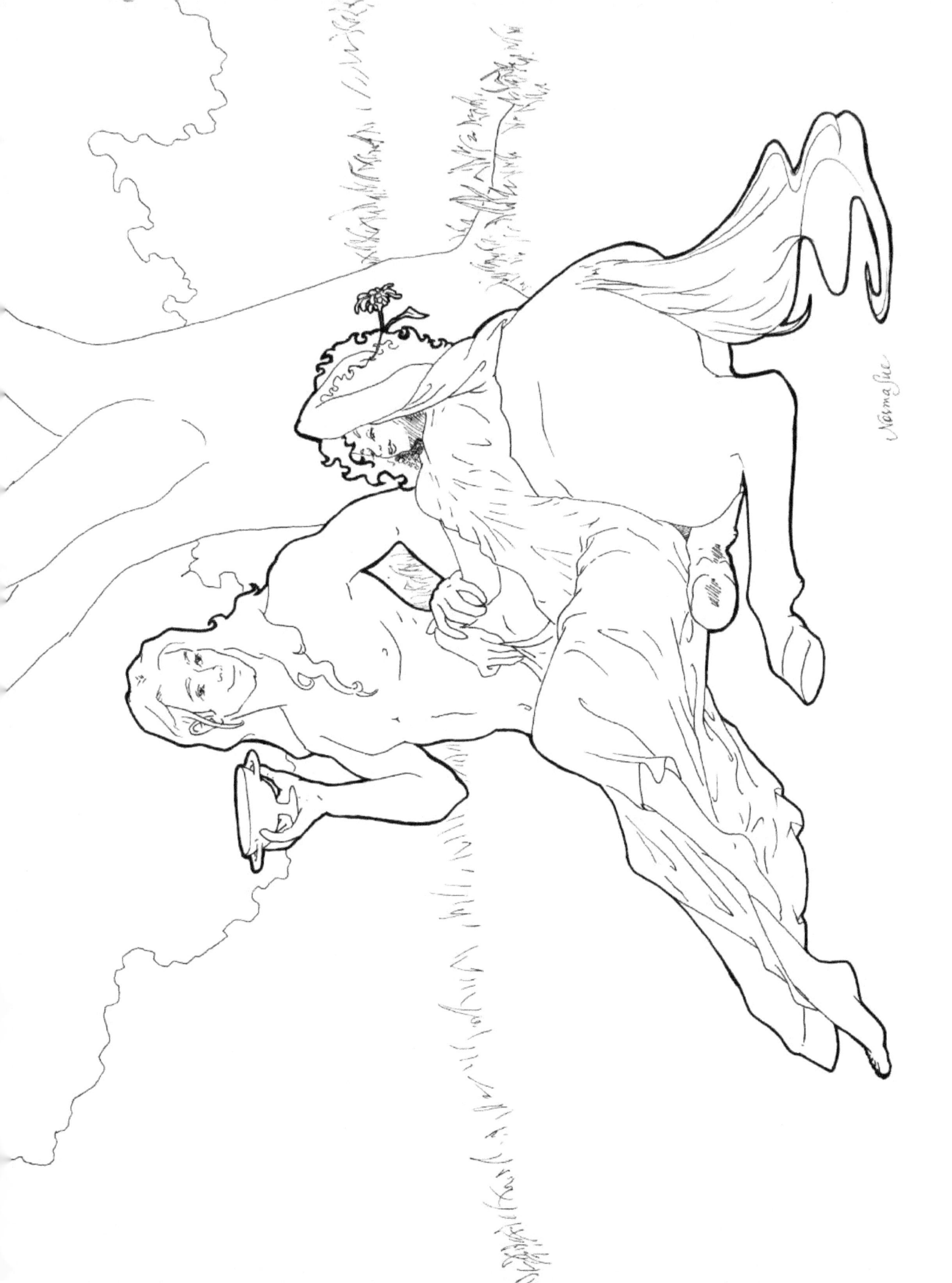

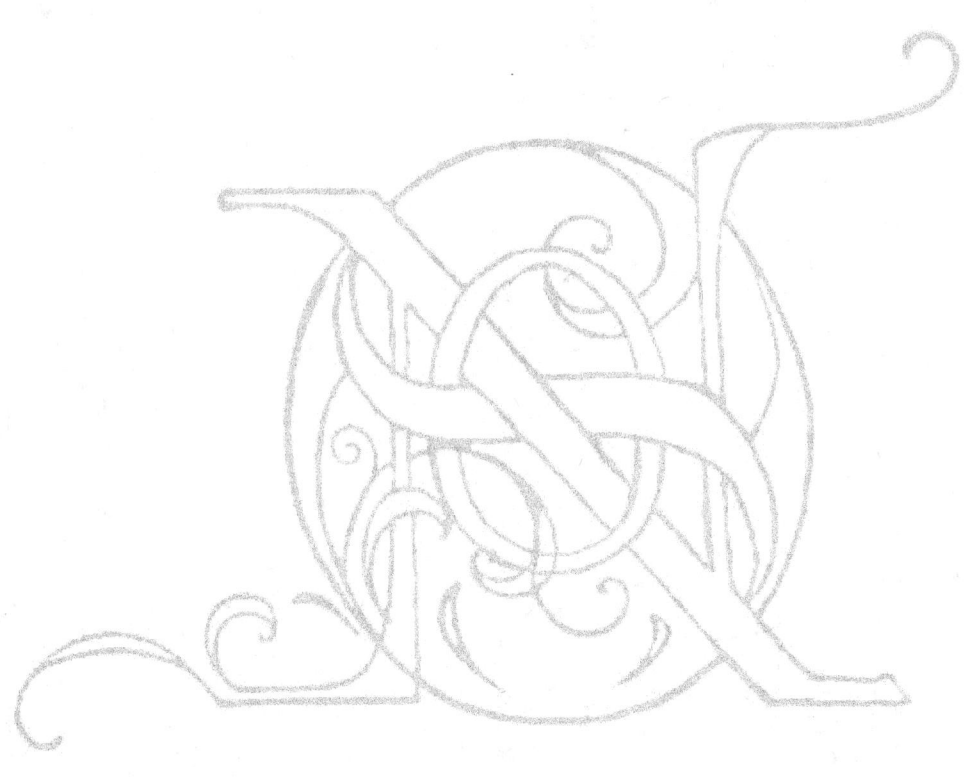

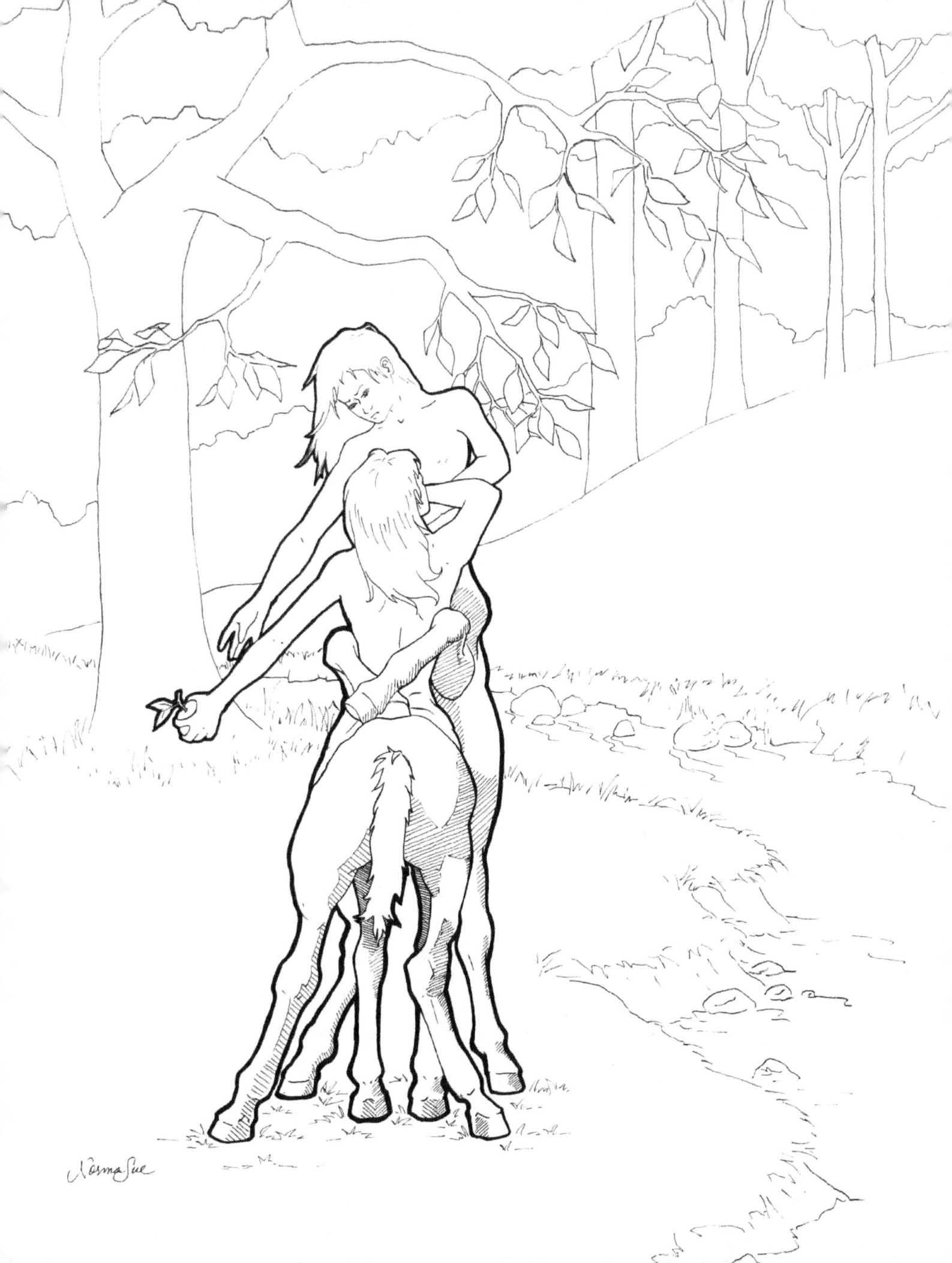

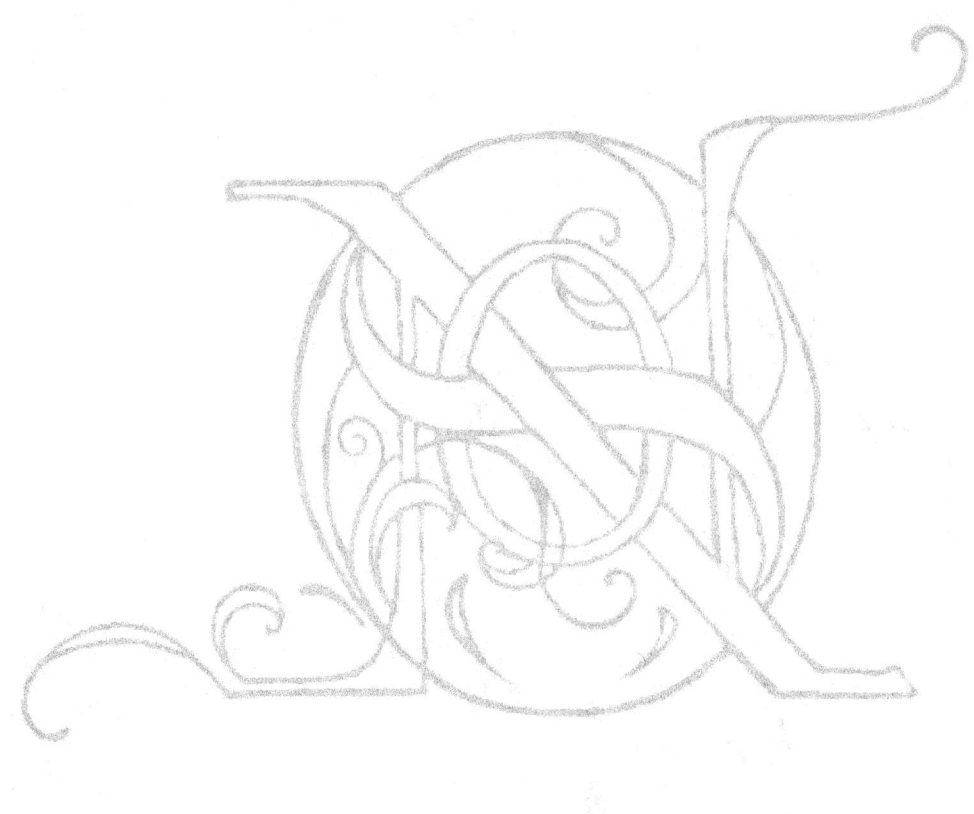

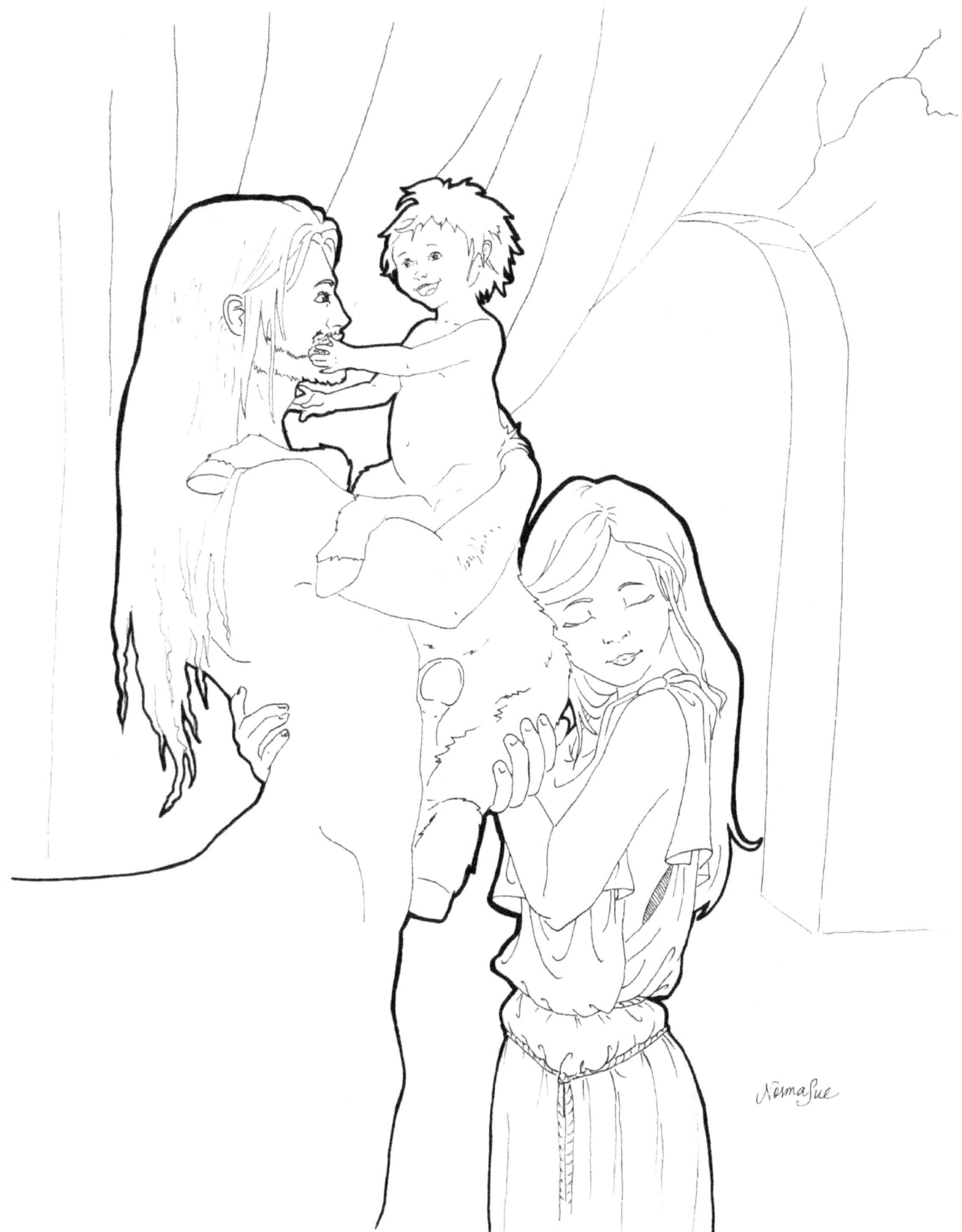

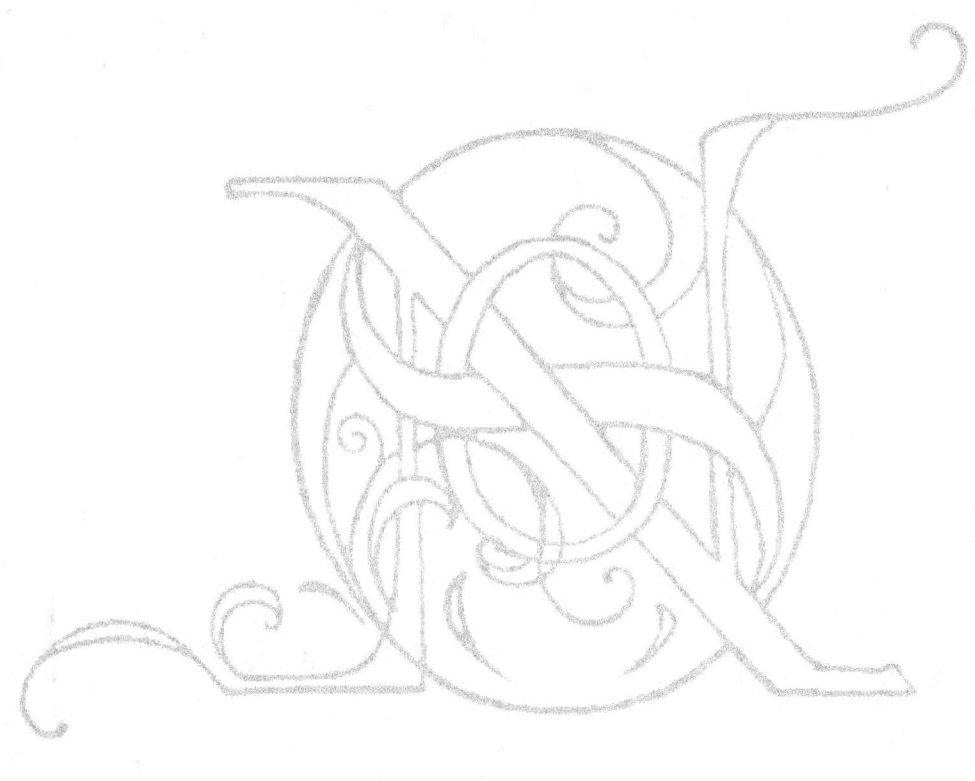

www.ingramcontent.com/pod-product-compliance
Lightning Source LLC
Chambersburg PA
CBHW062236220526
45471CB00009B/3510